A Concise Guide
to
MLA
Documentation
and Style

Thomas Fasano

COYOTE CANYON PRESS

www.coyotecanyonpress.com

For information about obtaining permission to reprint material from this book, send your request by e-mail (info@coyotecanyonpress.com) or fax (1-800-319-4707).

Library of Congress Cataloging-in-Publication Data Available

ISBN-13: 978-0-9821298-1-4
ISBN-10: 0-9821298-1-5

First printing August 2009

Book set in Times Ten, Lucida Sans, and Gill Sans

Published by Coyote Canyon Press
Claremont, California
www.coyotecanyonpress.com

Contents

Foreword

I wrote this book for my students after failing to find a book that adequately simplified the MLA documentation style. In addition I wanted a classroom text that would make MLA style easier for my students to understand. In the years since my undergraduate days, a seismic shift has taken place in the way students conduct research, find primary and secondary sources, gather and store information, and write their research papers. To accommodate these changes in research methodologies, the MLA guidelines have grown in length, number, and complexity with the result that many students struggle to understand even the basics of MLA style. Students using this book can rest assured that it was teacher designed and student tested in the classroom, where my eleventh-graders helped me see immediately what needed improving. Because of their involvement, the strengths of this book are theirs; its weaknesses, mine.

This book is not a publication of the Modern Library Association, nor does it bear any endorsement from the association. For a longer and more thorough presentation of the topics presented in this book, the reader should consult the following MLA publications: the *MLA Handbook for Writers of Research Papers*, 7th edition, in which the MLA style of documentation is exhaustively detailed; and the *MLA Style Guide to Scholarly Publishing*, 3rd edition, whish is aimed at an audience of graduate students and professional scholars writing for publication. Information can also be found on the MLA Web site: http://www.mla.org.

Tom Fasano
July 9, 2009

MLA Style

The Modern Language Association (MLA) has established and promoted a citation style used throughout the humanities. Instead of traditional footnotes and endnotes, it uses parenthetical citations such as (Mencken 328). Parenthetical citations should be as brief as possible. For example, to cite an entire book, just insert (Mencken) at the end of a sentence, or (Mencken 27) to refer to page 27. You can also omit the citation entirely if you've made the author and title clear in your writing and you are not citing any particular passage.

Complete information about each citation appears at the end of the research paper in a bibliography entitled **Works Cited** (see fig. 1). The purpose of parenthetical citations is to direct the reader to specific entries in the works-cited list, which like other bibliographies contains three necessary types of information: author, title, and publication data.

1. Formatting the Paper

The List of Works Cited

In an MLA-style research paper, the list of works cited is the only place a reader will find complete bibliographic information about the sources used in the writing of the paper. For that reason the list must be as complete and accurate as possible. In other words, the list of works cited is where you tell your readers what sources you used in your research and where exactly in those sources you found the material.

The list of works cited comes at the end of your paper and includes only the sources from which you quoted, paraphrased, summarized, or to which you made reference. Occasionally instructors will require a list of all the sources you consulted during your research, not just the ones you actually cited, in which case use the term **Works Consulted**. The MLA Handbook prefers the terms **Works Cited** or **Works Consulted** instead of the older Bibliography ("description of books") since research papers today are likely to include many more types of media than just books.

What follows are some basic guidelines for preparing the list of works cited:

1. Paginate the list of works cited continuously with the rest of the essay. If the last page of your essay begins on page 7, begin your list of works cited on page 8 (see fig. 1).

2. Double-space the list of works cited, flush left with a hanging indent of one-half inch (see fig. 1).

3. Alphabetize the list of works cited by author. For anonymous works, alphabetize them by title instead. Ignore but do not delete articles: *A, An,* and *The.*

CURRENT RECOMMENDATIONS, MLA 7th EDITION

4. Works published independently are *italicized*: books, plays, long poems published as books, pamphlets, newspapers, magazines, journals, films, radio and television programs, Web sites, CDs, software, ballets, operas, paintings, and other works and artifacts that stand on their own.

5. List the medium of publication for every entry in the list of works cited. For example: Richardson, Robert D. *Emerson: The Mind on Fire*. Berkeley: U of California P, 1995. Print. Or: Schwarz, Benjamin. "California Dreamers." *TheAtlantic.com*. July 2009. Web. 7 July 2009.

6. The guidelines in the MLA Handbook no longer recommend that URLs be included in the list of works cited unless requested by an instructor.

7. One of the biggest changes in the 7th edition of the MLA Handbook concerns how to cite Web pages whose data appear in other media. For example, you may need to give bibliographic information for a book scanned in for viewing on the Web or a film available both on DVD and as streaming video (see pp. 15–16).

8. When citing two or more works by the same author, give the name in the first entry only. For the second and subsequent entries, in place of the name, type three hyphens and a period before the title. The three hyphens act as a substitute for the author's name.

9. Use appropriate abbreviations for publishers' names (*Scribner's* for *Charles Scribner's Sons*). See the list of abbreviations on page 38.

10. Capitalize all significant words in titles and subtitles, ignoring the original capitalization. Unless they begin the title or subtitle, do not capitalize articles (*a, an, the*), prepositions (*of, to, in, against*), coordinating conjunctions (*and, but, for, nor, or, so, yet*), and the *to* in infinitives (*to run, to dance*).

11. The titles of works published within other works are typically placed within quotation marks. These include articles, essays, stories, short

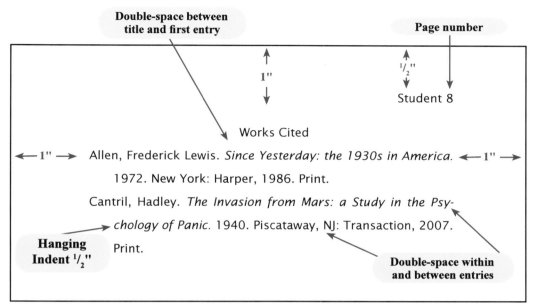

Double-space between title and first entry

Page number

1"

$\frac{1}{2}$"

Student 8

Works Cited

←—1"—→ Allen, Frederick Lewis. *Since Yesterday: the 1930s in America.* ←—1"—→

1972. New York: Harper, 1986. Print.

Cantril, Hadley. *The Invasion from Mars: a Study in the Psy-*

chology of Panic. 1940. Piscataway, NJ: Transaction, 2007.

Hanging Indent $\frac{1}{2}$" Print.

Double-space within and between entries

Fig. 1. The top of the first page of a list of works cited.

poems, chapters, encyclopedia entries, sections of online documents, songs, and individual episodes of broadcast programs.

12. Italicize a title that would normally be italicized when it appears within a title requiring quotation marks: "Buddhist Thought in *Siddhartha*."

13. Enclose in single quotation marks a title requiring quotation marks when it appears inside another title that also requires quotation marks: "Ironic Reversal in Robert Frost's 'Stopping by Woods on Snowy Evening.'"

14. Italicized titles within italicized titles require no italics: *Racism Denied:* Adventures of Huckleberry Finn *as Mirror of Twain's Beliefs*.

15. Enclose in quotation marks a title normally requiring quotation marks when it appears within an italicized title: *"The Purloined Letter" and Poe's Invention of Form*.

16. Titles of sacred works like the Bible and the Koran are not italicized. Nor are the names of laws or other political documents (the U.S. Constitution).

17. The divisions of a work are not italicized (preface, introduction, foreword, act, scene, canto, section, etc.) Nor are they capitalized when they occur in the text of the paper.

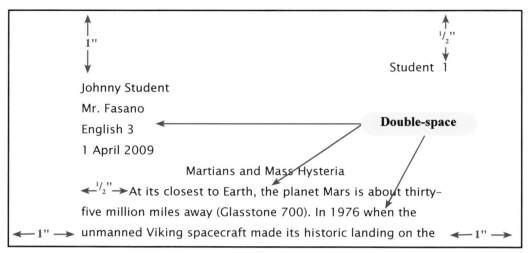

Fig. 2. The top of the first page of a research paper.

The Body of the Paper

1. Essays should be stapled or paper clipped in the upper left corner. Most instructors don't like binders or plastic covers, so don't use then. Print essays on white 8½ x 11 paper.

2. Print on only one side of the page in black ink. Use a readable typeface such as Times Roman, which has a high contrast between roman and italic styles. The MLA guidelines call for italicizing titles instead of underlining them; therefore, a font with a high contrast between roman and italics is crucial.

3. At the top of the first page of your essay, one inch below the top edge, type your name, your instructor's name, the course number (including the section number), and the due date. Put each on a separate line (see fig. 2).

4. Margins should be one inch on all four sides (except for page numbers). Double-space the essay throughout (including indented quotations and the list of works cited) with no extra spaces between paragraphs. The first line of each paragraph should be indented an additional half-inch. Paragraphs are flush left (see fig. 2).

5. Starting with the first page, create a running head with page numbers a half-inch from the top edge of the paper, flush with the right-hand margin. Type your last name before the page number (Fasano 1). All pages are numbered (see fig. 3).

6. The title of your research paper should not be italicized or put in quotation marks. If you are using the title of a book or a quotation for your title, then format those words accordingly. As a convention

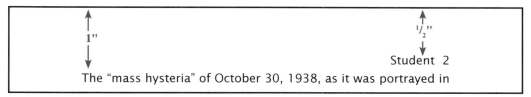

Fig. 3. The running head of a research paper.

of style, your title should signal what your essay is about: Smashing the Idols: The Rise of Christianity in Pagan Europe. Or: "Tell Stories with Grace": Reflections on the Theme of Providence in Marlowe. Or: The Breath of Dogs: Godless Death in *King Lear*. As you can see from these examples, titles often consist of two parts joined with a colon. Typically one part is creative and the other more specific.

2. Sample Entries: The List of Works Cited

The MLA Handbook has extensive guidelines for formatting sources in the list of works cited, including recommendations for an array of electronic and print media. The following models illustrate the kinds of sources most commonly used.

Nonperiodical Print Publications

The MLA Handbook uses the cumbersome phrase "nonperiodical print publications" to refer to **books** and **pamphlets**. When citing these, provide as much of the following information as possible:

> Author's last name, first name. *Book Title.* Additional information.
>
> City of publication: Publisher, publication date. Print.

Sample entries in this chapter are numbered for reference.

A Book by a Single Author

1. Powers, Thomas. *Heisenberg's War.* New York: Knopf, 1993. Print.

2. Fletcher, Richard. *The Barbarian Conversion: From Paganism to Christianity.* New York: Holt, 1997. Print.

3. Rowling, J[oanne] K[athleen]. *Harry Potter and the Order of the Phoenix.* New York: Levine-Scholastic, 2003. Print.

4. MacDonald, Ross [Kenneth Millar]. *The Galton Case.* 1959. New York: Warner, 1990. Print.

An Anthology

5. Oates, Joyce Carol, ed. *The Oxford Book of American Short Stories.* Oxford: Oxford UP, 1992. Print.

6. Mizener, Arthur, ed. *F. Scott Fitzgerald: A Collection of Critical Essays.* Englewood Cliffs, NJ: Prentice, 1963. Print.

A Book by Two or Three Authors

7. Beckson, Karl, and Arthur Ganz. *Literary Terms: A Dictionary.* New York: Farrar, 1989. Print.

A Book by Four or More Authors

8. Gilman, Sandra, et al. *Hysteria Beyond Freud.* Berkeley: U of California P, 1993. Print.

A Book by a Corporate Author

9. Pax World Investments. *Annual Report 2008.* Providence: Pax World, 2008. Print.

A Work in an Anthology

10. Thoreau, Henry David. *Walden, or Life in the Woods. The Norton Anthology of American Literature: Shorter Edition.* Ed. Ronald Gottsman, et al. New York: Norton, 1979. 585–705. Print.

11. Keats, John. "Ode to a Nightingale." *The Best Poems of the English Language.* Comp. Harold Bloom. New York: Harper, 2004. 463–65. Print.

An Article in a Reference Book

12. Meyendorff, the Rev. John. "Eastern Orthodoxy." *The New Encyclopaedia Britannica: Macropaedia.* 15th ed. 2002. Print.

13. Leiren, Terje. "Norway." *The Encyclopedia Americana.* 2004 ed. Print.

14. Donno, Elizabeth Story. "Varieties of Sixteenth-Century Narrative Poetry." *Columbia History of British Poetry.* Ed. James Shapiro. 1994. Print.

15. Nichols, Roger. "Francis Poulenc." *The New Grove Dictionary of Music & Musicians*. Ed. Stanley Sadie. 1980. Print.

An Introduction, a Preface, a Foreword, or an Afterword

16. Greenblatt, Stephen. Foreword. *Will in the World*. By Greenblatt. New York: Norton, 2004. 11-14. Print.

17. Faggen, Robert. Introduction. *Early Poems*. By Robert Frost. Ed. Robert Faggen. New York: Penguin, 1998. xi-xl. Print.

18. Schlosser, Eric. Preface. *The Jungle*. By Upton Sinclair. New York: Penguin, 2006. vii-xv. Print.

19. King, Stephen. Afterword. *Different Seasons*. By King. New York: Signet-Penguin, 1998. 501-08. Print.

A Book by an Anonymous Author

20. *Chase's Calendar of Events 2008*. 50th Anniversary Ed. New York: McGraw, 2008. Print.

A Scholarly Edition

21. Poe, Edgar Allan. *The Selected Writings of Edgar Allan Poe*. Ed. G. R. Thompson. New York: Norton, 2004. Print.

A Translation

22. Tolstoy, Leo. *Anna Karenin*. Trans. Rosemary Edmonds. London: Penguin, 1977. Print.

23. Pirandello, Luigi. *Six Characters in Search of an Author and Other Plays*. Trans. Mark Musa. London: Penguin, 1995. Print.

An Illustrated Book or a Graphic Narrative

24. Potter, Beatrix. *The Complete Tales*. Illus. Beatrix Potter. New York: Warne-Penguin, 2006. Print.

25. Copeland, Charles, illus. *Pinocchio: The Adventures of a Marionette*. By Carlo Collodi. Trans. Walter S. Cramp. Boston: Ginn, 1904. Print.

26. Collodi, Carlo. *Pinocchio: The Adventures of a Marionette.* Trans. Walter S. Cramp. Illus. Charles Copeland. Boston: Ginn, 1904. Print.

A Book Published in a Second or Subsequent Edition

27. Tyson, Lois. *Critical Theory Today: A User-Friendly Guide.* 2nd ed. New York: Routledge, 2006. Print.

A Multivolume Work

28. Caro, Robert A. *Master of the Senate.* New York: Knopf, 2002. Vol. 3 of *The Years of Lyndon Johnson.* 3 vols. to date. 1982–2004. Print.

29. Durant, Will, and Ariel Durant. *The Age of Voltaire.* New York: Simon, 1965. Vol. 9 of *The Story of Civilization.* 11 vols. 1935–75. Print.

A Book in a Series

30. Wilson, C. Philip, Charles C. Hogan, and Ira L. Mintz, eds. *Fear of Being Fat: The Treatment of Anorexia Nervosa and Bulimia.* New York: Aronson, 1983. Print. Classical Psychoanalysis and Its Applications.

A Republished Book or Publisher's Imprint

31. Kaplan, Justin. *Mr. Clemens and Mark Twain.* 1959. New York: Simon, 2006. Print.

32. Banks, Russell. *Continental Drift.* 1985. New York: Perennial-Harper, 2007. Print.

A Brochure, Pamphlet, or Press Release

33. *Cruise Guide 2009.* Los Angeles: Crystal Cruises, 2008. Print.

34. *Renoir Lithographs.* New York: Dover, 1994. Print.

35. Medical Marijuana Now. *Medical Marijuana Now Announces New Stores.* Los Angeles: MMN, 20 Apr. 2009. Print.

A Government Publication

36. United States. The President's Commission on the Assassination of President Kennedy. *Report of the President's Commission on the Assassination of President Kennedy.* Washington, DC: GPO, 1964. Print.

37. *Cong. Rec.* 25 Feb. 2009: 2656-706. Print.

38. Michigan. Dept. of Public Health. *Lifelines for Children: Child Mortality in Michigan.* Michigan: Lansing, 1989. Print.

Published Proceedings of a Conference

39. Kartiganer, Donald M., and Ann J. Abadie, eds. *Proceedings of Faulkner and Yoknapatawpha Conference: Faulkner at 100: Retrospect and Prospect, 27 July–1 August, 1997.* Jackson: UP of Mississippi, 2000. Print.

A Book Published Before 1900

40. Jahn, Otto. *The Life of Mozart.* Trans. Pauline D. Townsend. 3 vols. London, 1891. Print.

An Unpublished Dissertation

41. Franson, Robert T. "Women in Shakespeare's History Plays." Diss. U of Southern California, 1988. Print.

A Published Dissertation

42. Zimmerman, Robert. *Manuscript Revision in Byron's* Childe Harold's Pilgrimage. Diss. Duke U, 1960. Ann Arbor: UMI, 2001. Print.

Periodical Print Publications

When citing articles in periodicals—newspapers, magazines, journals—provide the following categories of information:

Author's last name, first name. "Article Title." *Periodical Title* Volume.Issue (Date): Inclusive pages. Print.

An Article in a Scholarly Journal

43. Ryan, Karen. "The Devil You Know: Postmodern Reconsiderations of Stalin." *Mosaic* 36.3 (2003): 87–111. Print.

44. Murphy, Karen L., Roseanne DePasquale, and Erin McNamara. "Meaningful Connections: Using Technology in Primary Classrooms." *Young Children* 58.6 (2003): 12–18. Print.

An Article in a Scholarly Journal Using Only Issue Numbers

45. Davis, William D., et al. "Using Sensor Signals to Analyze Fires." *Fire Technology* 39 (2003): 295–308. Print.

46. Weaver, Jesse. "John and Frank Craighead." *Wildlife Society Bulletin* 24 (1996): 767–69. Print.

47. Ranald, Ralph. "George Orwell and the Mad World: The Anti-Universe of 1984." *South Atlantic Quarterly* 66 (1967): 544–53. Print.

An Article in a Newspaper

48. Swed, Mark. "It's Frankly Scandinavian." *Los Angeles Times* 28 June 2009, late ed.: E6. Print.

49. Mathews, Anna Wilde. "When All Else Fails: Forcing Workers into Healthy Habits." *Wall Street Journal* 8 July 2009: D1+. Print.

An Article in a Magazine

50. Zakaria, Fareed. "Theocracy and Its Discontents." *Newsweek* 29 June 2009: 30–39. Print.

51. Ellroy, James. "My Mother's Killer." *GQ* Aug. 1994: 145+. Print

A Review

52. Banks, Eric. "Tossed About on an Unruly Sea." Rev. of *The Blue Hour: A Life of Jean Rhys*, by Lilian Pizzichini. *Los Angeles Times* 28 June 2009: E9. Print.

An Abstract in an Abstracts Journal

53. Stephenson, Denise R. "Blurred Distinctions: Emerging Forms of Academic Writing." Diss. U of New Mexico, 1996. *DAI* 57 (1996): item 1700A. Print.

An Anonymous Article

54. "Goings on About Town." *New Yorker* 23 Feb. 2009: 7. Print.

An Editorial

55. "Inquiring Minds." Editorial. *Los Angeles Times* 28 June 2009: A35. Print.

56. Alter, Jonathan. "One Nation Under Medicare." Opinion piece. *Newsweek* 29 June 2009: 24. Print.

57. Gall, Bret, and Steve Simpson. "The Media and the First Amendment." Opinion piece. *Wall Street Journal* 13 July 2009: A11. Print.

A Letter to the Editor

58. Chaidez, Sam. Letter. *Los Angeles Times* 2 July 2009: A28. Print.

A Serialized Article

59. Fiore, Faye, and Mark Z. Barabak. "Obama Begins Leading America in a New Direction." *Los Angeles Times* 19 Apr. 2009, final ed.: A1+. Print. Pt. 1 of a series, Ambition and Audacity.

60. Fiore, Faye, and Peter Wallsten. "Getting to know the Obamas, on Their Terms." *Los Angeles Times* 20 Apr. 2009, final ed.: A1+. Print. Pt. 2 of a series, Ambition and Audacity, begun 19 Apr. 2009.

61. McManus, Doyle. "Measuring Obama by FDR's Yardstick." *Los Angeles Times* 21 Apr. 2009, final ed.: A1+. Print. Pt. 3 of a series, Ambition and Audacity, begun 19 Apr. 2009.

Web Publications

Citations of Web publications have a lot in common with those of print publications. Most Web publications have an author, a title, and publication information, just like print sources. In the case of online sources, because Web sites are constantly updated, scholars need to record the date of last access in addition to the medium of publication.

Formerly the MLA Handbook recommended including URLs of Web sites in works-cited lists. In practice inclusion of URLs proved to be less helpful than intended. Because readers can easily find sources on the Web by typing names and titles into a search engine, you should include a URL only if your reader is unlikely to find the source or if your instructor requires it. Enclose URLs in angle brackets < > followed by a period. Break long URLs after a slash. Give the complete URL, including *http*.

When citing Web publications, provide the following information:

> Author's last name, first name. Name of editor. "Article Title." or
> *Book Title*. Print publication information if previously pub-
> lished. *Title of Web site*. Publisher or sponsor of site, or N.p.
> if name is not available. Date of publication, or n.d. if not
> available. Medium of publication (Web). Date of access. URL,
> if required.

Online Collections

62. Halsall, Paul, ed. *Internet Medieval Sourcebook*. Fordham University Center for Medieval Studies, 10 Dec. 2006. Web. 9 Apr. 2009.

Interview

63. Morrison, Van. Interview by Tim Morrison. *Time.com*. Time Inc., 26 Feb. 2009. Web. 9 Aug. 2009.

Music Sample

64. Jeremy Denk, perf. "Piano Sonata No. 1." By Charles Ives. *Ojai Music Festival*. Ojai Music Festival, 2009. Web. 7 July 2009.

Encyclopedia Entry

65. "Defoe, Daniel." *Encyclopaedia Britannica Online*. Encyclopaedia
    Britannica, 2009. Web. 9 Aug. 2009.

Author's Project Page

66. Warren, Craig A., ed. *The Ambrose Bierce Project*. Penn State U,
    2009. Web. 29 June 2009.

Bibliography

67. Moïse, Edwin E., comp. *Vietnam War Bibliography*. Clemson U, 27
    June 2009. Web. 17 July 2009.

Radio News Segment

68. "Madoff Sentenced To Maximum 150 Years In Prison." *National
    Public Radio*. Natl. Public Radio, 28 June 2009. Web. 29 June
    2009.

Blog or Personal Site

69. Martin, Paul L. "Education by Humiliation." *The Teacher's View*.
    N.p., 5 June 2009. Web. 6 June 2009.

Map

70. "Claremont, California." Map. *Google Maps*. Google, 29 Mar. 2009.
    Web. 29 Mar. 2009.

News Article from Broadcasting Company

71. Walker, Matt. "Lion Prides Form to Win Turf Wars." *BBC*. British
    Broadcasting Company, 29 June 2009. Web. 7 July 2009.

Magazine Article

72. Ross, Alex. "The Storm of Style." *The New Yorker*. Condé Nast Digi-
    tal, 24 July 2006. Web. 10 Aug. 2009.

Newspaper Article

73. Alini, Erica. "No More Perks: Coffee Shops Pull the Plug on Laptop Users." *WSJ.com.* Dow Jones & Company, Inc., 8 Aug. 2009. Web. 9 Aug. 2009.

Newspaper Editorial

74. "Focus on Results, Not Treatments." Editorial. *Los Angeles Times.* Los Angeles Times, 29 June 2009. Web. 29 June 2009.

Television News Segment

75. Banoun, Annick. "Hook Me Up: Free Starbucks Ice Cream." *KNBC.com.* KNBC, 7 July 2009. Web. 9 July 2009.

Academic Department Page

76. "The Simple Past or Imperfect Tense (das Präteritum)." Chart. *A Review of German Grammar.* Dept. of German Studies at Dartmouth, 18 Feb. 2009. Web. 14 Mar. 2009.

Megapage

77. Baragona, Alan, narr. "To Rosemounde." By Geoffrey Chaucer. *Chaucer Metapage.* Ed. Mark E. Allen, et al. U of North Carolina, 21 Aug. 2008. Web. 21 May 2009.

Wiki, i.e., Wikipedia

78. "Jimi Hendrix." *Wikipedia, The Free Encyclopedia.* 12 Aug. 2009, 17:22 UTC. Wikimedia Foundation, Inc. 13 Aug. 2009.

Web Sites with Print Publication Data

If you need to cite a work that also appeared in print, include the bibliographic data of its print publication. For example, a print publication that was scanned into *Google Book Search* would be cited in this way (see next entry).

79. Grey, Zane. *Riders of the Purple Sage.* Illus. Douglas Duer. New
York: Grosset, 1912. *Google Book Search.* Web. 12 Apr. 2009.

80. Kylliäinen, Janne. "Living Poetically in the Modern Age: The Situ-
ational Aspects of Kierkegaard's Thought." Diss. U of Helsinki,
2009. *E-Thesis Helsinki.* Web. 15 June 2009.

81. Kelly, Dorothy. *Reconstructing Woman: Gender and Scientific
Thought in Nineteenth-Century French Narrative.* University
Park: Pennsylvania State UP, 1997. *Penn State Romance Studies.*
Web. 29 June 2009.

82. Herodotus. *The Histories.* Trans. A. D. Godley. Cambridge: Harvard UP, 1920. *The Perseus Digital Library.* Ed. Gregory Crane.
Tufts U. Web. 12 Mar. 2007.

83. Whitman, Walt. "When Lilacs Last in the Dooryard Bloom'd."
Washington DC, 1871. *The Walt Whitman Archive.* Web. 29 June
2009.

Web Sites with Publication Data for Other Media Besides Print

Some Web sites have data which appear in other media. For example, you
may be need to give bibliographic information for a book scanned in for
viewing on the Web (see above section) or a film available both on DVD
and as streaming video (see *Night of the Living Dead* below).

The Web abounds with images (still and moving) and audio, thereby
making it necessary to indicate that a source online is something other
than text. Thus, if you viewed a digitized version of a movie, you should
include in your list of works cited the appropriate information for a film
citation.

84. *Night of the Living Dead.* Dir. George Romero. 1968. *Internet Archive.* Web. 12 Apr. 2009.

85. Bellows, George. *Cliff Dwellers.* 1913. Los Angeles County Museum
of Art. *Modern Urban America.* Web. 30 June 2009.

86. Evans, Walker. *Graveyard and Steel Mill.* 1935. Prints and Photo-
graphs Div., Lib. of Cong. *Farm Security Administration—Office
of War Information Collection.* Web. 29 June 2009.

87. "Milton's Mysterious Dream." 1816-20. *The William Blake Archive.*
    The Pierpont Morgan Lib. *Illustrations to Milton's "L'Allegro" and*
    "Il Penseroso." Web. 30 June 2009.

Web-Based Scholarly Journals

As with print periodicals, most scholarly journals published exclusively on the Web are cataloged by volume number, issue number, and the date of publication. A Web-based scholarly journal probably won't include page numbers, so in most instances use *n. pag.* in place of inclusive page numbers.

88. Brown, Marshall. Rev. of Scott's *Shadow: The Novel in Romantic Ed-*
    inburgh, by Ian Duncan. *Romanticism and Victorianism on the*
    Net 53 (2009): n. pag. Web. 30 June 2009.

89. Masciandaro, Nicola. "Black Sabbath's 'Black Sabbath': A Gloss on
    Heavy Metal's Originary Song." *Reconstruction* 9.2 (2009): n.
    pag. Web. 1 July 2009.

Web Publications in Online Databases

Some databases gather articles from various periodicals. Often these are library subscription databases.

90. Leigh, David J. "Narrative, Ritual, and Irony in Bunyan's *Pilgrim's*
    Progress." *Journal of Narrative Theory* 39.1 (2009): n. pag. *Proj-*
    ect Muse. Web. 11 July 2009.

91. Brophy, Thomas J. "On Church Grounds: Political Funerals and
    the Contest to Lead Catholic Ireland." *The Catholic Historical*
    Review 95.3 (2009): n. pag. *Project Muse.* Web. 7 July 2009.

92. Jepson, Edgar. "The Literary and Economic Future of Liberal Mor-
    monism." *The English Review* Apr. 1909: 172-78. *The Modernist*
    Journals Project. Web. 30 June 2009.

93. Goldman, David. "Martians Invade New Jersey! Orson Welles' Great
    Halloween Scare." *Biography* Oct. 2000: 28+. *SIRS Researcher.*
    Web. 24 Feb. 2009.

Additional Common Sources

A Television or Radio Broadcast

94. "Arvo Pärt's Timeless Twist on Tradition." Narr. Tom Manoff. *All Things Considered.* Natl. Public Radio. KPCC, Pasadena, 5 Mar. 2009. Radio.

95. *Satyagraha.* By Philip Glass. Perf. Rachelle Durkin, Richard Croft, Earle Patriarco, and Alfred Walker. Metropolitan Opera. Cond. Dante Anzolini. *The Metropolitan Opera International Radio Broadcast.* WQXR-FM, New York, 11 Apr. 2008. Radio.

96. "Van Gogh." *Power of Art.* Narr. Simon Schama. Dir. David Belton. PBS. KCET, Los Angeles, 18 June 2008. Television.

97. "Wallander." By Henning Mankell. Perf. Kenneth Branagh. 3 episodes. *Masterpiece Mystery.* Introd. Alan Cumming. PBS. KCET, Los Angeles, 10 May–31 May 2009. Television.

98. Welles, Orson, dir. "The War of the Worlds." By H. G. Wells. Adapt. Howard Koch. *Mercury Theatre on the Air.* CBS Radio. WCBS, New York, 30 Oct. 1938. Radio.

A Sound Recording

99. Bach, Johann Sebastian. *Matthäus-Passion: Arias and Choruses.* Perf. Kiri Te Kanawa, Anne Sofie von Otter, Anthony Rolfe Johnson, and Tom Krause. Chicago Symphony Chorus and Chicago Symphony Orchestra. Cond. Sir Georg Solti. Rec. Mar. 1987. London, 1988. CD.

100. Davis, Miles. *Kind of Blue.* Perf. Miles Davis, Julian Adderley, John Coltrane, Wyn Kelly, Bill Evans, Paul Chambers, and James Cobb. Rec. 2 Mar. and 22 Apr. 1959. Columbia, 1959. LP.

101. Zorn, John. *Spillane.* Nonesuch, 1987. CD.

102. Miller, Arthur. *The Crucible.* Perf. The Repertory Theatre of Lincoln Center. Caedmon, 1998. Audiocassette.

103. Iron Maiden. "Rime of the Ancient Mariner." By Steve Harris. *Powerslave.* EMI, 1984. CD.

104. Welles, Orson, dir. *The War of the Worlds.* By H. G. Wells. Adapt. Howard Koch. Rec. 30 Oct. 1938. Evolution, 1969. LP.

A Film or a Video Recording

105. *Once.* Dir. John Carney. Fox Searchlight, 2007. Film.

106. Schrader, Paul, writer. *Taxi Driver.* Dir. Martin Scorsese. Perf. Robert De Niro, Jodie Foster. 1976. Columbia TriStar Home Video, 1999. DVD.

107. *It's a Wonderful Life.* Dir. Frank Capra. Perf. James Stewart, Donna Reed, Lionel Barrymore, and Thomas Mitchell. 1946. Republic, 2001. DVD.

108. Kurosawa, Akira, dir. *Rashomon.* Perf. Toshiro Mifune. 1950. Home Vision, 2001. Videocassette.

A Performance

109. *Hamlet.* By William Shakespeare. Dir. John Gielgud. Perf. Richard Burton. Shubert Theatre, Boston. 4 Mar. 1964. Performance.

110. *Phantom of the Opera.* By Andrew Lloyd Webber. Dir. Tom None. Winter Garden, New York. 13 Aug. 1988. Performance.

111. *Hay Fever.* By Noel Coward. Dir. Robert Fryer. Ahmanson Theater, Los Angeles. 8 Apr. 1983. Performance.

112. *The Barber of Seville.* By Gioachino Rossini. Libretto by Cesare Sterbini. Dir. Javier Ulacia. Cond. Michele Mariotti. Perf. Daniela Nathan Gunn, Juan Diego Flórez, and Joyce DiDonato. LA Opera, Los Angeles. 29 Nov. 2009. Performance.

A Musical Score or Libretto

113. Schikaneder, Emanuel. *The Magic Flute.* 1791. Composed by Wolfgang Amadeus Mozart. English version by Ruth and Thomas Martin. New York: Schirmer, 1971. Print.

114. Beethoven, Ludwig van. *Symphony No. 7 in A, Op. 92.* 1812. New York: Dover, 1998. Print.

A Work of Visual Art

115. Tolone, Robert. *Tree Trimmer, Manhole Man, and Garbage Man.* 2005–06. Public Art. City Yard, Claremont, CA.

116. Gainsborough, Thomas. *The Blue Boy.* 1770. Oil on canvas. Huntington Library, San Marino, CA.

117. Evans, Walker. *Penny Picture Display.* 1936. Photograph. Museum of Mod. Art, New York.

An Interview

118. Glass, Philip. "Philip on Film: New York-London." *Looking Glass.* Dir. Eric Darmon. Ideale Audience, 2005. DVD.

119. Caro, Robert. Interview by Brian Lamb. *Q & A.* C-SPAN2. 4 Jan. 2009. Television.

120. Del Toro, Guillermo. Interview. *Los Angeles Times* 2 July 2009: D1+. Print.

A Map or Chart

121. "Cape Hatteras to Straits of Florida." Map. *Marine Waypoints.* 2 July 2009. Web.

122. *California.* Map. Chicago: Rand, 1992. Print.

A Cartoon or a Comic Strip

123. Warp, Kim. Cartoon. *New Yorker* 15 Dec. 2008: 56. Print.

124. Miller, Wiley. "Non Sequitur." Comic strip. *Los Angeles Times* 2 July 2009: D18. Print.

An Advertisement

125. Ally Bank. Advertisement. *CNN.* 1 July 2009. Television.

126. Abbott Laboratories. Advertisement. *Newsweek* 29 June 2009: 5–7. Print.

A Lecture, a Speech, an Address, or a Reading

127. Benedict, Barbara. "The Adventures of Count Boruwlaski, an
       18-Century Polish Dwarf." Trinity College, Hartford. 16 March
       2006. Lecture.

128. Hyman, Earle. "Reading of Shakespeare's *Othello*." Symphony
       Space, New York. 28 Mar. 1994. Speech.

129. Terkel, Studs. Conf. on Coll. Composition and Communication
       Convention. Palmer House, Chicago. 22 Mar. 1990. Address.

A Letter, a Memo, or an E-Mail Message

130. Douglass, Frederick. "To William Lloyd Garrison." 26 Feb. 1846.
       Rpt. in *Life and Writings of Frederick Douglass*. Ed. Philip Foner.
       Vol. 1. New York: International Publishers, 1950. 138. Print.

131. Delillo, Don. Letter to the author. 2 Feb. 2001. TS.

132. Winkler, David. "Loneliness of the Long Distance Runner." Message
       to the author. 30 Apr. 2009. E-mail.

A Legal Source

133. Aviation and Transportation Security Act. Pub. L. 107–71. 115 Stat.
       597–647. 19 Nov. 2001. Print.

134. Dist. of Col. v. Heller. 554 US 1–147. Supreme Court of the US.
       2007. *Supreme Court Collection*. Legal Information Inst., Cornell
       U Law School, n.d. Web. 2 July 2009.

An Article on Microform (Microfilm, Microfiche)

135. Purvis, Andrew. "The Sins of the Fathers." *Time* 26 Nov. 1990.
       Microform. NewsBank: Welfare and Social Problems 12 (1990):
       fiche 1, grids A29–31.

A Nonperiodical Publication on CD-ROM or DVD-ROM

136. *The World's Best Poetry on CD*. CD-ROM. Vers. 2.0. Roth, 1996.
       CD-ROM.

137. Myers, Alfred S. "Houdini, Harry." *Collier's Encyclopedia CD-ROM: Unabridged Text Version*. Vers. 1.0. Collier, 1997. CD-ROM.

138. *Exploring Shakespeare*. CD-ROM. Vers. 1.0. Detroit: Gale, 1997. CD-ROM.

Material from a Periodically Published Database on CD-ROM or DVD-ROM

139. Jacobs, Paul. "New Process Helps Scientists Sort Crucial Genes." *Los Angeles Times* 4 Nov. 1999: C2. *CD News*. CD-ROM. News-Bank. Dec. 1999.

A Digital File

140. Buena Park High School. "Disciplinary Referral Process." *Student Handbook*. Buena Park, CA: N.p., 2008. PDF file.

141. Hansard, Glen, perf. "All the Way Down." *Once: Music from the Motion Picture*. Columbia, 2007. MP3 file.

3. Citing Sources in the Text

Parenthetical Citations

You need to tell your readers what sources you consulted in your research and where exactly you found them. To do this, insert a brief parenthetical citation wherever you have used the words and/or ideas of someone else. Usually this type of citation includes the author's last name and the page number of the reference. The following three examples demonstrate parenthetical citations at their most basic:

1. Enclose in parentheses the author's last name followed by the page number(s).

One historian argues that the pastor of Salem Village, "the Reverend Samuel Parris, had become the focal point of considerable discontent, which his actions in the coming months would magnify, rather than dampen" (Norton 16).

2. Use the author's last name in your sentence and enclose the page number in parentheses.

Norton points out that "whether because strife in the Village came to focus on the church or because the Villagers made inappropriate choices of clergymen, each of the four ministers who served the Village failed to earn consistent support from his parishioners" (3–4).

3. Use only the author's last name in your sentence with no parenthetical citation. Use this method when referring to an entire work.

Norton argues for a new interpretation of the witchcraft crisis, one that is rooted in the context of a specific time and place, Essex County, Massachusetts, in the 1690s.

The above parenthetical citations point to the following entry in the list of works cited:

Works Cited

Norton, Mary Beth. *In the Devil's Snare: The Salem Witchcraft Crisis of 1692.* New York: Vintage-Random, 2003. Print.

Placement of Parenthetical Citations

For the sake of readability, the MLA Handbook recommends placing parenthetical citations at the end of sentences before the final period. Notice too that there is no punctuation between the author's name and the page number.

In *The Great Gatsby* the romantic relationships put on display "a pattern of behavior grounded in the characters' fear of intimacy, the unconscious conviction that emotional ties to another human being will result in one's being emotionally devastated" (Tyson 39).

Occasionally you may want to place the parenthetical citation within your sentence to make the quotation a more integral part of your flow of words.

Tyson suggests that "the interest created by the romance between Gatsby and Daisy lies not in its apparent uniqueness" (39) but in the way it reflects all the dysfunctional relationships in the novel.

If a quotation extends to more than four lines, set it off from the rest of the text with an additional one-inch left margin and place the parenthetical reference after the final period (see p. 31 for a further explanation).

Lois Tyson's description of the dysfunctional characters in *The Great Gatsby* establishes that their entanglements drive the plot forward:

> For a psychoanalytic reading, however, the interest created by the romance between Gatsby and Daisy lies not in its apparent uniqueness but in the ways in which it mirrors all the less appealing romantic relationships depicted—those between Tom and Daisy, Tom and Myrtle, Myrtle and George, and Nick and Jordan—and thereby reveals a pattern of psychological behavior responsible for a good deal of the narrative progression. (39)

Works Cited

Tyson, Lois. *Critical Theory Today: A User-Friendly Guide.* 2nd edition. New York: Routledge, 2006. Print.

Parenthetical Citations: Examples

Occasionally you will need to modify the basic format for parenthetical citations. The examples below illustrate common situations that require such modifications.

Each example concludes with an entry that would be included in a list of works cited.

1. Citing Part of a Work with Section Numbers

If quoting from specific passages in a source with sections, give the appropriate section (e.g. paragraph) numbers in your parenthetical citation.

"If Platter," according to Sohmer, "is describing a performance at the Globe of Shakespeare's *The Tragedy of Julius Caesar*, this evidence marks 21 September 1599 as the latest date on which the theater could have opened" (par. 5).

Works Cited

Sohmer, Steve. "12 June 1599: Opening Day at Shakespeare's Globe." *Early Modern Literary Studies* 3.1 (1997): 46 pars. Web. 26 Mar. 2009.

2. Citing volume and page number of a multivolume work

If you are citing a volume from a multivolume work, include in your parenthetical citation the specific number of the volume you are referring to.

At the end of the war, "public opinion was mainly fixed on the fighting in Virginia, where the casualties had been awesome from the start" (Foote 3: 375).

Works Cited

Foote, Shelby. *The Civil War: A Narrative.* 3 vols. New York: Random, 1974. Print.

3. Citing a work listed by title

Alphabetize anonymous works by the first important word in the title. The full title (if short) or a shortened form of it replaces the author's last name in the parenthetical citation. Begin shortened titles with the word by which the source is alphabetized.

Cohen published his first book of poems, *Let Us Compare Mythologies,* in 1956. He went on to write several more books, including the ground-breaking novel *Beautiful Losers* "before Judy Collins launched his music career with her 1966 rendition of his mystical, yearning love song 'Suzanne'" ("Goings").

Works Cited

"Goings on About Town." *New Yorker* 23 Feb. 2009: 7. Print.

4. Citing a work by a corporate author

To cite a work by a corporate author, you may include the corporate name within parentheses (Pax World). It is better, however, to include a long name in your sentence, especially if you are citing several corporate authors in one text.

Pax World Investments' annual report claims that there are huge lessons to be learned from the current financial crisis, primarily that the business world must come to terms with the fact that corporations have been "transformed into vehicles whose primary purpose becomes making a small group of management insiders enormously rich over very short periods of time" (1).

Works Cited

Pax World Investments. *Annual Report 2008.* Providence: Pax World, 2008.

5. Citing two or more works by the same author

One way to do this is to place a comma after the author's last name, add a shortened form of the title, and then supply the page number(s). Another possibility is to include the author's last name and title within the body of your sentence and then enclose the page number(s) in parentheses at the end of the sentence.

There was much conflict in the Johnson household concerning Lyndon's college career (Caro, *Path* 123).

Caro argues in *Means of Ascent* that Johnson stole the 1948 senatorial election in Texas by 87 votes (317).

Works Cited

Caro, Robert A. *Means of Ascent.* 1990. New York: Vintage-Random, 1991. Print.

- - -. *The Path to Power.* 1982. New York: Vintage-Random, 1990. Print.

6. Citing Indirect Sources

If possible, find material in its original source, but occasionally the only source available is an indirect one. For example, the author of a source you're using might have included a quotation from another author's work. In such instances use the abbreviation *qtd. in* before the source in the parenthetical citation.

Larsen writes, "Today's librarian is part teacher, part entrepreneur" (qtd. in Brown 424).

Works Cited

Brown, J. D. "Librarians as Business People: A Review of the Literature." *Journal of For-Profit Librarianship* 28 (2006): 421–436. *Academic Search Premier.* Web. 16 March 2008.

You also might use a quotation that contains a quote within in it. Although you don't need to cite the source of the quoted quote, your readers might benefit if you explain the origin of the original source in a footnote.

David M. Kennedy writes that Roosevelt tried to strike a confident chord "by reassuring his countrymen that 'this great nation will endure as it has endured, will revive and will prosper. . . . The only thing we have to fear . . . is fear itself.'"[17]

[17]Kennedy, *Freedom from Fear.* The Roosevelt quote comes from his first inaugural address in 1933.

7. Citing common literature

The MLA Handbook recommends providing enough information to locate the quotation in any edition of the work. After the page number, type a semicolon and use abbreviations to specify the chapter (*ch.*), book (*bk.*), paragraph (*par.*), section (*sec.*), scene (*sc.*), and so on.

Stephen Crane allowed that the mind of a soldier might "cast off its battlefield ways and resume its accustomed course of thought" (107; ch. 14).

Works Cited

Crane, Stephen. *The Red Badge of Courage.* New York: Norton, 1976. Print.

For prose plays give the page number followed by a semicolon, then act and scene numbers.

Early in *Death of a Salesman*, Miller has Willy Loman wonder that a man can "work a lifetime to pay off a house. . . . and then there's nobody to live in it" (1241; act 1, sc. 1).

When citing verse plays and poems, omit page numbers and cite by division. Give the act, scene, and line numbers in arabic numerals separated by periods. (*Macbeth* 2.1.44-45).

8. Citing more than one work in a single parenthetical citation

When including two or more works in a single parenthetical citation, separate each citation with a semicolon.

(Anderson 18; Coxe 131)

Works Cited

Anderson, Wallace L. *Edwin Arlington Robinson: A Critical Introduction.*
Cambridge: Harvard UP, 1968. Print.

Coxe, Louis O. *Edwin Arlington Robinson: The Life of Poetry.* New York:
Pegasus, 1969. Print.

4. Footnotes and Endnotes

The MLA Handbook recommends the use of notes for two purposes:

1. Content notes for information that cannot easily fit into the text
2. Bibliographic notes for citing additional sources

Place a superscript arabic numeral after the reference in the text and include the information in a footnote or endnote.

1. Content Notes: for information that cannot easily fit into the text

Poe's "Al Aaraaf" runs much longer than any poem he ever penned.[1]

Note

[1] The poem runs to 422 lines, which is four times the length that Poe himself later thought advisable.

2. Bibliographic Notes: for citing additional sources

Poe's invention of the modern detective story derives from his chronic despair and was an act of personal consolation.[1]

Note

[1] For a useful explanation of Poe's creative process see Silverman 171–74 and Hoffman 104–15.

Works Cited

Hoffman, Daniel. *Poe, Poe, Poe, Poe, Poe, Poe, Poe.* New York: Doubleday,
1972. Print.

Silverman, Kenneth. *Edgar A. Poe: Mournful and Never-Ending Remem-*
brance. New York: Harper, 2009. Print.

5. Considerations for Your Research

The starting point for most research nowadays is not the local library but the World Wide Web. To some this statement might seem blasphemous, but it's true: students today are more likely to go straight to Google or Wikipedia than to a library catalog, which is not a bad way to *begin* your research. Unfortunately, many students never get past this initial stage.

Locating Sources of Information

Knowing where to look for information is the key to effective research. Scholarly sources, which are peer reviewed (read by expert readers), used to be available only in print but are now increasingly likely to be found online. Yet locating print sources does not necessarily mean making a trip to the library. Today, many libraries make their information available through a variety of online sources such as electronic catalogs, databases, and library homepages, all of which function as portals to a vast sea of information.

For the student researcher, wading through so much information can be overwhelming. Just knowing where to start requires an understanding of the different types of print and electronic sources at your fingertips and what they have to offer. For example, the library may not be the best source of up-to-the-minute information, but most online sources won't offer the kinds of in-depth scholarly analysis provided by the books and printed journals found in most libraries.

Types of Sources

1. **Scholarly books and articles.** Written by scholars and rigorously peer reviewed, they take time to produce and may not represent the most current thinking in their respective fields.

2. **Serious books and articles.** Written by experts and professional writers and reviewed by editors, they are usually more current than scholarly books and articles.

3. **Popular magazines.** Written by professional writers and journalists, they are most often current but may not be the most in depth.

4. **Newspapers.** Written by journalists and reviewed by editors, they are very current but may not be thorough.

5. **Sponsored Web sites.** Information is reviewed by the sponsor to ensure its suitability for the sponsor's purpose.

6. **Individual Web sites.** Written by almost anyone, they range in subject matter, and their authority varies widely.

7. **Listservs and newsgroups.** Using a mailing list software application, a virtual community of users—students, laypersons, or experts—can send emails to all subscribers on the "list"; content may or may not be moderated; newsgroups, unlike listservs, allow anyone to post.

8. **Blogs and wikis.** Written by anyone from individuals to experts and scholars, they may be reviewed, commented upon, or updated by subsequent readers, and their source information might be documented or linked; like individual Web sites, their authority varies widely.

9. **Online databases.** Written mainly by scholars, they carry the same weight as printed scholarly books and articles.

Evaluating Sources

Most scholarly work published in print format has gone through a rigorous peer-review process. Unfortunately, the same cannot be said about other types of sources. Therefore, researchers need to determine the reliability of the information they collect from their research. If a source cannot be substantiated, you will need to verify the original or find an additional source to substitute for it. The MLA Handbook recommends that researchers concentrate on the *authority, accuracy,* and *currency* of their sources in order to judge their reliability.

1. **A source should be authoritative.** Researchers must ask themselves if a source has been "peer reviewed." Most scholarly journals and academic book publishers engage in peer review, a process by which publishers consult with experts about a piece before publishing it. Also, the author's credentials lend credibility to the work. Does the author have the requisite education and training in the field or relevant experience to give the work credence? You can reasonably judge the authority of a book since most books are reviewed by experts as well as commented upon online. Look to see what others have said about the book before making up your mind. For Web sites check the "About the Author" or "About Us" links. If no author is listed (a bad sign) look for information about any sponsoring organization. Most Web sites associated with academic institutions post material that's been read by experts or gone over by an editor. Unfortunately, numerous Web sites are maintained by individuals whose expertise is doubtful. Keep in mind that most of the information on individual sites is never edited, verified, or fact checked.

2. **A source should be accurate.** Check to see if the work's sources are listed. The titles and authors in the list of works cited will tell you about the breadth of the author's research and about any possible bias. Web publications almost always provide hyperlinks to their sources as a means for readers to verify their claims. Be leery of Web sites whose links are mostly broken or cite individual pages and not academic or

scholarly sites.

3. **A source should be current.** Good researchers rely on the most current work in their respective fields. To determine currency, look for either publication and copyright dates or dates of last update or revision. Print publications have copyright dates printed on the copyright page, and online sources usually list the date of last update at the bottom of the front page. Keep in mind that many Web sites are not updated frequently and may be out of date. Also, checking the dates of any listed sources can help determine how current a Web site is. Note, too, that most reputable sites will give an e-mail address or comment box for you to contact the author or sponsoring organization with any questions you might have.

Compiling Sources and Taking Notes

In today's world the computer is the writing instrument of choice, but many researchers still use index cards to record all information acquired during their research—bibliographic data on one side and quotations, summaries, paraphrases, etc. on the other. The cards are handy and provide all the information needed to compile a list of works cited. Another effective means of conducting research is to write notes and marginalia on photocopies or printouts of your sources. If doing things the old-fashioned way is not for you, try creating separate word-processed files to keep track of all bibliographic information and content notes. No matter how you store the information, your collection of cards, printouts, files, etc. will be essential to keeping track of your research. Eventually, you will compile a provisional works-cited list, without which a successful paper will be almost impossible.

It is imperative that this provisional list be in place *before* you begin the actual writing of your paper. You will no doubt expand and refine your list as you proceed in your writing, but without this provisional list you will have no clue as to your sources or how to document those sources. You will be lost.

Quoting Sources

Quotations must be used selectively, or they lose their impact. Use only quotations that stand out and are interesting in some vivid and relevant way. Also, aim for brevity with quotations. Long quotations and the overuse of them will bore your readers and peg you as a sloppy scholar or lazy thinker—or both.

When omitting words from the middle of a sentence, use ellipses (three spaced periods) with a space before and after each period.

To make your text flow smoothly, use one of the following methods of integrating quotations:

1. Integrate the quoted passage into the flow of your sentence.

Gass points out that three of Wittgenstein's older brothers were suicides and "an early death must have seemed the inherited fate of the family" (148).

2. Set the stage for a quoted passage with an introductory sentence followed by a colon.

People who knew him have tried to reconcile the brilliant mind with the stubborn, arrogant attitude: "I am inclined to believe it was not Wittgenstein's brilliance by itself that impressed Moore, Russell, Keynes . . . but the fact that he did indeed burn with a bright, gemlike flame" (Gass 151).

3. Set off a quoted passage (four or more lines) with an introductory sentence followed by a colon.

This method is used for long quotations of four or more lines. Double-space the quotation and indent it one inch from the left margin. There is no need to use quotation marks. Notice that the final period goes *before* the parenthetical citation instead of *after* it. There should be a single space after the period. If the quotation extends to more than one paragraph, the first line of each paragraph should have an additional indent of a quarter inch.

William Gass, in "At Death's Door: Wittgenstein," explains how the high rate of suicide in Vienna shaped the overall mind-set of the young philosopher:

> In those days, if music appeared to be the rosy flush of Vienna's fame, suicide seemed its fever. The newsworthy surface of society was regularly ruffled by someone's dramatically premature demise. There was Otto Weininger, whose crackpot book *Sex and Character* Wittgenstein, in his early years, admired; Ludwig Boltzmann, important for his work in statistical dynamics, and one with whom, equally early, Wittgenstein wished to study in Vienna; the poet Georg Trakl; notables like the archi-

tect of the Imperial Opera House, Eduard van der Null; aristo-

crats of a rank as elevated as the Baron Franz von Uchatius,

including actual imperialities such as the Crown Prince Rudolf

himself—each a distinguished suicide. (146)

4. Set off poetry with either slashes or an introductory sentence followed by a colon.

Use quotation marks to set off two or three lines of verse, with a slash and a space on either side (/) to separate them.

Robert Frost points out an ironic reversal between nature and time

when he writes, "The woods are lovely, dark and deep. / But I have

promises to keep, / And miles to go before I sleep" (86).

If quoting verse of more than three lines, begin the quote on a new line and indent the passage one inch from the left margin. Place a parenthetical citation at the end of the last line.

MIlton's "Lycidas" opens with the swain (shepherd) grieving for the

death of his friend:

Yet once more, O ye Laurels, and once more

Ye Myrtles brown, with Ivy never-sear

I com to pluck your Berries harsh and crude,

And with forc'd fingers rude,

Shatter your leaves before the mellowing year. (651)

Summarizing and Paraphrasing Sources

Summarizing and paraphrasing are two of the most powerful tools of research. Often these two terms are used interchangeably to mean a restatement of someone else's words, but they actually designate two different skills. To *summarize* is to condense the content of a long passage, that is, to capture its meaning in as few words as possible. In other words a *summary* is an accurate recasting of the original source's main points, support, and logic. A *paraphrase* is a restatement of the original passage, phrase by phrase, in your own words, and is much longer than a summary. These two skills will benefit you greatly in your research.

Remember, all summaries and paraphrases you write are yours, and because you own them you do not have to enclose them in quotation marks. However, since the ideas your are restating are someone else's, you need to cite the source in your research paper.

What follows are two common methods of integrating summaries and paraphrases into your paper:

1. A Summary of a long quotation (see the Gass quotation on pp. 31–32).

Include the author's name in the body of your sentence and enclose the page number(s) in parentheses, thereby informing your reader that you are summarizing someone else's writing.

Award-winning writer William Gass argues that the social climate of Vienna made it not a coincidence that many of the intellectuals and writers Wittgenstein admired the most committed suicide (146).

2. A Paraphrase of a short quotation (see the third sentence of the Gass quotation).

Paraphrasing is an effective method of establishing the authority of the author if you have previously quoted from the source. In addition it helps you avoid cluttering your paper with too many quotations. Simply enclose the author's name and page number(s) in parentheses at the end of the sentence.

Suicide was not an uncommon event in Wittgenstein's Vienna (Gass 146).

Works Cited

Gass, William. "At Death's Door: Wittgenstein." *Finding a Form.* New York: Knopf, 1997.

Plagiarism: What It Is and How to Avoid It

Plagiarism is stealing. It is passing someone else's writing and ideas off as your own without giving appropriate credit. Whether you do this intentionally or unintentionally, it is a serious offense, a breach of academic honesty, and can earn you an F in your course—or even worse. To help you avoid plagiarizing, the following suggestions should prove helpful:

1. Accurately document your sources whenever you use the following:

   • A direct quote

   • A summary or paraphrase of someone else's words

2. Take notes as carefully and accurately as you can. Whether you use notecards or store everything on your computer, be sure to identify the source of *every passage* in your notes.

3. Use your sources as *support* for your ideas, logic, and writing rather than as a *substitute* for them.

The following excerpt is from Mary Beth Norton's *In the Devil's Snare*, an account of the Salem witchcraft hysteria of 1692. The first two examples (Versions A and B) illustrate how a student committed plagiarism either by repeating the author's words and ideas or borrowing an entire passage from the original. The last example (Version C) demonstrates how the student avoided plagiarism by properly citing and documenting the source.

Original Version

Even on the very day of his examination Burroughs did not cease his spectral activity. He pinched Goody Vibber's arm as she was en route to the Village for the examination; never having met him before, she could not identify his apparition until she saw him in person later.

Version A (repeating an author's words and ideas)

On the same day of his examination Burroughs failed to stop his spectral activity. The townsfolk noticed that he pinched Goody Vibber's arm as she was headed toward the Village for the examination. She had never met him before, and she could not identify his apparition until she saw him in person later.

Version A is plagiarism. The writer has tried to pass off the words and ideas of another as her own and has failed to indicate that they belong to Mary Beth Norton. The writer has stolen these words and ideas.

Version B (borrowing an entire passage)

Mary Beth Norton points out that even on the very day of his examination Burroughs did not cease his spectral activity. He pinched Goody Vibber's arm as she was en route to the Village for the examination; never having met him before, she could not identify his apparition until she saw him in person later (151).

Version B is also plagiarism. Even though the writer cites her source and includes a parenthetical citation, she has borrowed an entire passage from the original and failed to use quotation marks to indicate the extent of her borrowing. Her readers will think she wrote this.

Version C

Mary Beth Norton argues that on the day Salem's former minister, the Rev. George Burroughs, was examined by the court, some in the town believed that his specter was active in the township: "He pinched Goody Vibber's arm as she was en route to the Village for the examination; never having met him before, she could not identify his apparition until she saw him in person later" (151).

Version C avoids plagiarism by using the source material properly. The writer has identified her source, thereby letting the reader know from whom she quoted. She explains the importance of the passage in her own words, then quotes from the original. She ends by providing a parenthetical citation.

Works Cited

Norton, Mary Beth. *In the Devil's Snare: The Salem Witchcraft Crisis of 1692.* New York: Vintage-Random, 2003. Print.

6. Abbreviations

Introduction

Use abbreviations primarily in the list of works cited. In the text of your paper, you'll rarely use abbreviations (except with parenthetical citations). When using abbreviations, be sure to follow the recommended forms listed below.

The MLA Handbook tends to recommend abbreviations without periods or spaces between them. Abbreviations made up of all capital letters are generally not followed by periods; those that end in lowercase letters are usually followed by periods.

Common Scholarly Abbreviations

app.	appendix
bk.	book
cf.	compare (does not mean "see")
ch., chap.	chapter
col.	column
comp.	compiler, compiled by
cond.	conductor, conducted by
conf.	conference
dir.	director, directed by
diss.	dissertation
doc.	document
ed.	editor, edition, edited by
et al.	and others
etc.	and so forth
fac.	faculty
facsim.	facsimile
fig.	figure
illus.	illustrator, illustration, illustrated by
misc.	miscellaneous
MS, MSS	manuscript, manuscripts
n, nn	note, notes (used after page numbers: "126n")
narr.	narrator, narrated by
n.d.	no date of publication
no.	number
n.p.	no publisher or place of publication indicated
n. pag.	no pagination
P	Press
p., pp.	page, pages (use only if needed for clarity)
par.	paragraph
perf.	performer, performed by
proc.	proceedings

prod.	producer, produced by
pseud.	pseudonym
pt.	part
qtd.	quoted
rept.	report, reported by
rev.	review, reviewed by
sc.	scene
sec.	section
ser.	series
st.	stanza
trans., tr.	translator, translated by
TS, TSS	typescript, typescripts
U	University (part of a publisher's name)
univ.	university
var.	variant
vers.	version
vs., v.	versus, *v.* for legal cases

Time Designations

Words representing units of time are spelled out in the text but abbreviated in the list of works cited. Abbreviate the months of the year, except May, June, and July. Some time designations are used only as abbreviations (a.m., p.m., AD, BC).

AD	after the birth of Christ, Latin *anno Domini*
BC	before Christ
a.m.	before noon, Latin *ante meridiem*
p.m.	after noon, Latin *post meridiem*
hr.	hour
Jan.	January
Feb.	February
Mar.	March
Apr.	April
Aug.	August
Sept.	September
Oct.	October
Nov.	November
Dec.	December
Sat.	Saturday
Sun.	Sunday
Mon.	Monday
Tues.	Tuesday
Wed.	Wednesday
Thurs.	Thursday
Fri.	Friday

Selected Publishers

Abbreviations are commonly used in the list of works cited for publishers' names. If the publisher's name includes the name of one person (Alfred A. Knopf), cite the surname only (Knopf). Should the publisher's name include more than one person's name (Harper and Row), use only the first one (Harper).

Abrams	Harry N. Abrams, Inc.
Allyn	Allyn and Bacon, Inc.
Basic	Basic Books
Cambridge UP	Cambridge University Press
Dodd	Dodd, Mead and Co.
Doubleday	Doubleday and Co., Inc.
Farrar	Farrar, Straus and Giroux, Inc.
Gale	Gale Research, Inc.
GPO	Government Printing Office
Harcourt	Harcourt Brace
Harper	HarperCollins
Harvard UP	Harvard University Press
Holt	Holt, Rinehart and Winston, Inc.
Houghton	Houghton Mifflin Co.
Knopf	Alfred A. Knopf, Inc.
Lippincott	J. B. Lippincott Co.
Little	Little, Brown and Company, Inc.
Macmillan	Macmillan Publishing Co., Inc.
McGraw	McGraw-Hill, Inc.
MIT P	The MIT Press
Norton	W. W. Norton and Co., Inc.
Oxford UP	Oxford University Press
Princeton UP	Princeton University Press
Random	Random House, Inc.
St. Martin's	St. Martin's Press, Inc.
Scribner's	Charles Scribner's Sons
Simon	Simon and Schuster, Inc.
St. Martin's	St. Martin's Press, Inc.
UMI	University Microfilms International
U of Chicago P	University of Chicago Press
UP of Mississippi	University Press of Mississippi
U of California P	University of California Press
Viking	The Viking Press, Inc.
Yale UP	Yale University Press

Index

Notes

Notes

LaVergne, TN USA
11 August 2010
192979LV00001B

9 780982 129814